✳ Your words Matter:

We're thrilled to embark on this journey with you, and we'd like to ask for a special favor that will help grow this community.

✦ The Power of Your Words:

Your opinions are crucial. If our book has resonated with you, we kindly ask you to share your experience by writing a review on Amazon. Your voice can inspire other readers and help us build an even stronger community.

✳ Constructive Feedback:

If you believe there's room for improvement or have suggestions on how to make "Human Anatomy Adult Coloring Book" even more impactful, we're eager to hear from you! Please send your thoughts to postmaster@beyondlastpage.com. We want this book to best meet your needs, and we're open to every suggestion.

🙏 The Importance of Amazon KDP Reviews:

Reviews are the lifeblood of Amazon KDP. Every word you write matters and can influence other readers. You're helping us grow and reach more people with "Human Anatomy Adult Coloring Book". Your review isn't just feedback; it's a supportive act that will help ensure this book reaches those who can benefit from it the most.

Link to reviews ⟶

Thank you from the bottom of our hearts for being part of our community and for sharing your journey towards a brighter future with "Human Anatomy Adult Coloring Book". ♥✨

Table of Contents

1 - Cranium

2 - Mandible

3 - Clavicle

4 - Humerus

5 - Ribcage

6 - Thoracic vertebrae

7 - Pelvis

8 - Sacrum

9 - Femur

10 - Patella

11 - Tibia

12 - Fibula

13 - Cervical vertebrae

14 - Scapula

15 - Sternum

16 - Thoracic vertebrae

17 - Radius

18 - Ulna

The bones of the human body

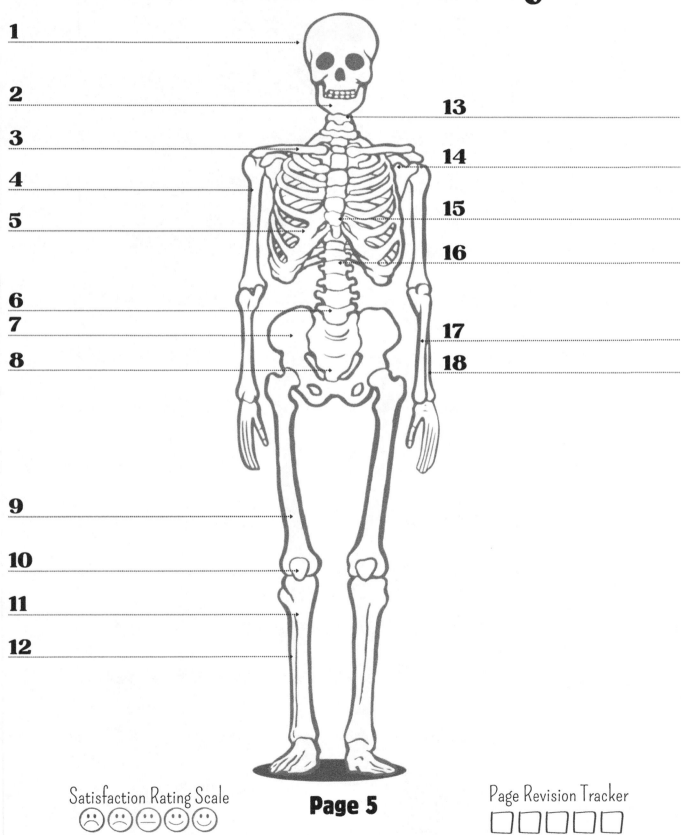

1 ....

2 ....

3 ....

4 ....

5 ....

6 ....

7 ....

8 ....

9 ....

10 ....

11 ....

12 ....

13 ....

14 ....

15 ....

16 ....

17 ....

18 ....

Satisfaction Rating Scale
☹ ☹ 😐 🙂 😊

Page Revision Tracker
☐ ☐ ☐ ☐ ☐

1 - Sphenoid bone

2 - Lacrimal bone

3 - Frontal bone

4 - Nasal bones

5 - Maxilla

6 - Mandible

7 - Parietal bone

8 - Temporal bone

9 - Zygomatic bone

10 - Zygomatic process

11 - Occipital bone

12 - Ear canal

13 - Mastoid process

14 - Styloid process

15 - Zygomatic arch

16 - Infraorbital foramen

17 - Supra orbital foramen

18 - Eye orbit

19 - Mental foramina

20 - Mandibular angle

21 - Alveolar margin

22 - Cornoid process

23 - Posterior condyle

Cranium

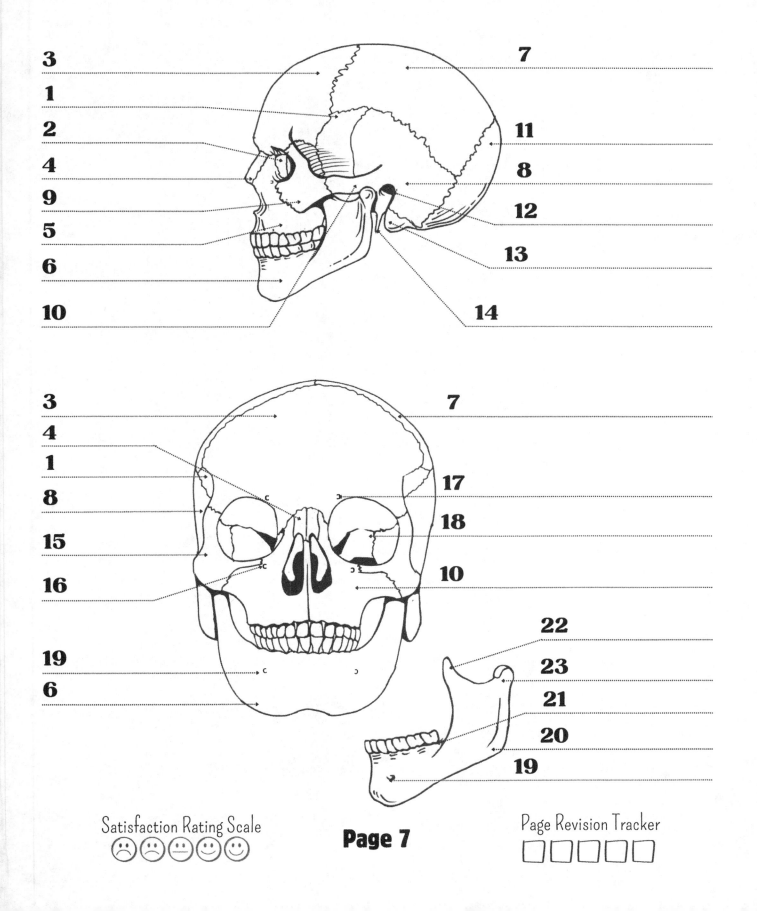

3

1

2

4

9

5

6

10

7

11

8

12

13

14

3

4

1

8

15

16

19

6

7

17

18

10

22

23

21

20

19

1 - Hard palate

2 - Soft palate

3 - Uvula

4 - Molars

5 - Premolars

6 - Canine

7 - Incisor

8 - Oral vestibule

9 - Superior labial frenulum

10 - Gum

11 - Palatoglossal arch

12 - Fauces

13 - Palatopharyngeal arch

14 - Tongue

15 - Gum

16 - Inferior lip

Dental system

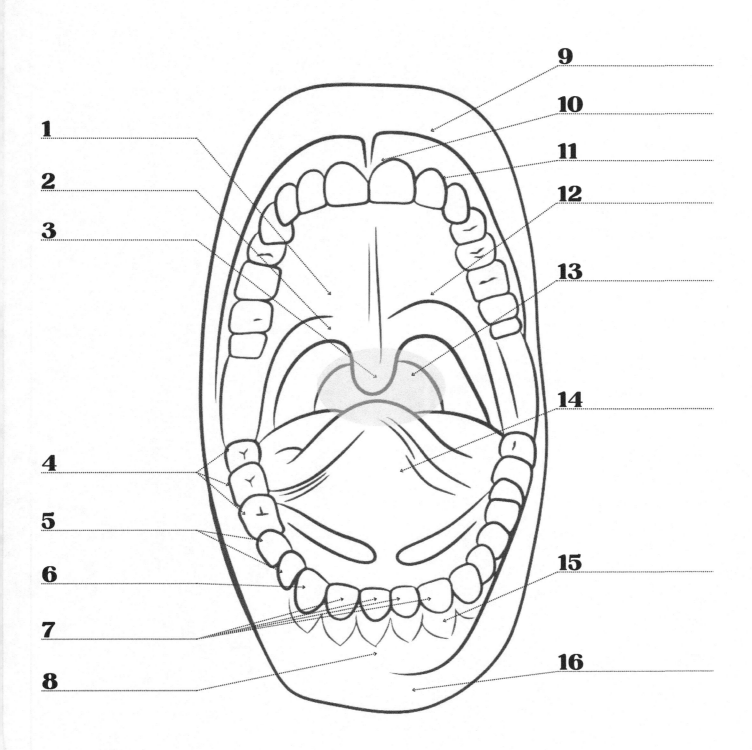

1

2

3

4

5

6

7

8

9

10

11

12

13

14

15

16

1 - Enamel
2 - Dentin
3 - Pulp cavity
4 - Gum
5 - Crown
6 - Neck
7 - Root
8 - Root canal
9 - Cementum
10 - Apical foramina

Tooth anatomy

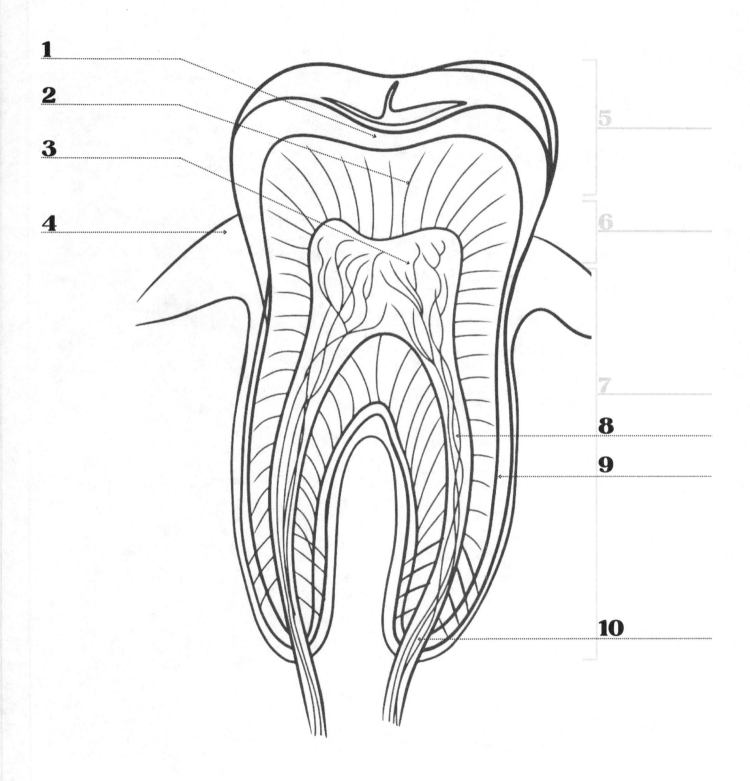

1

2

3

4

5

6

7

8

9

10

1 - **Acromial process**
2 - **Coracoid process**
3 - **Scapula notch**
4 - **Superior border**
5 - **Glenoid cavity**
6 - **Lateral border**
7 - **Medial border**
8 - **Supraspinous fossa**
9 - **Spine**
10 - **Infraspinous fossa**
11 - **Body**

Scapula

anterior view

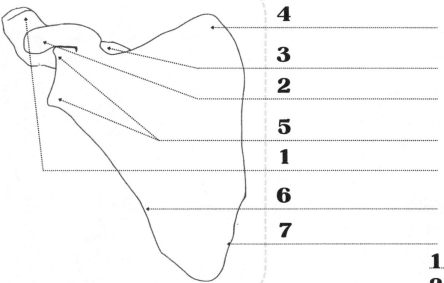

4
3
2
5
1
6
7

1
2
9
5
6

posterior view

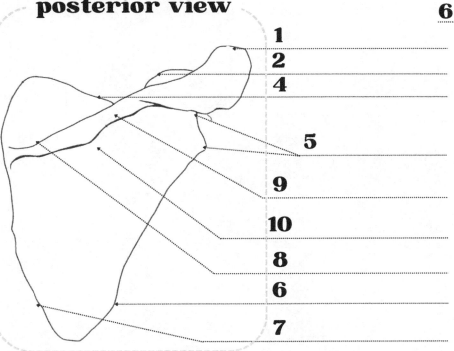

1
2
4

5

9

10

8

6

7

1 - **Cervical vertabrae c1-c7**
2 - **Thoracic vertabrae t1-t12**
3 - **Lumbar vertabrae l1-l12**
4 - **Iliac bone**
5 - **Asis**
6 - **Sacroiliac bone**
7 - **Sacroiliac joint**
8 - **Sacrum**

Vertebral column

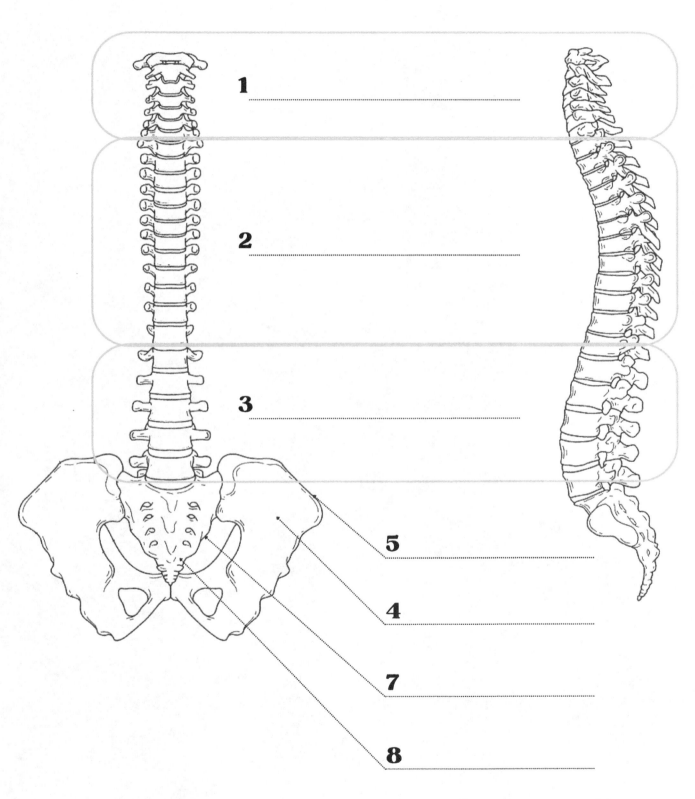

1 ....

2 ....

3 ....

5 ....

4 ....

7 ....

8 ....

1 - **Spinous process**
2 - **Laminae**
3 - **Articular process**
4 - **Transverse process**
5 - **Pedicle**
6 - **Body**
7 - **Superior articular process**

Vertebrae

1

2

3

4

5

6

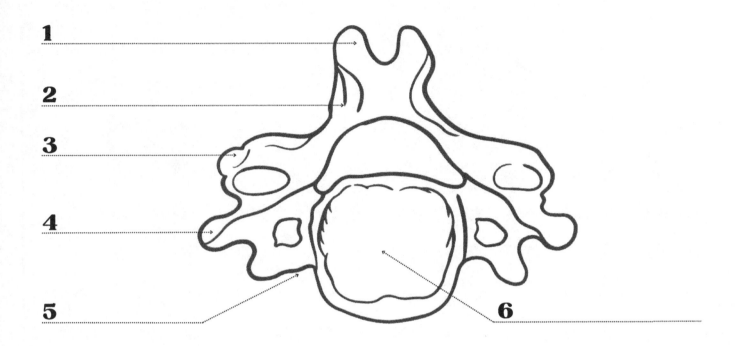

7

4

6

1

1 - Clavicles
2 - 1st rib
3 - Costal cartilages
4 - Sternocostal joints
5 - 10th rib
6 - Floating ribs
7 - Jugular notch
8 - Manubrium of the sternum
9 - Body of the sternum
10 - Xiphoid process of the sternum
11 - Costochondral joints
12 - Xiphisternal joint

Rib cage

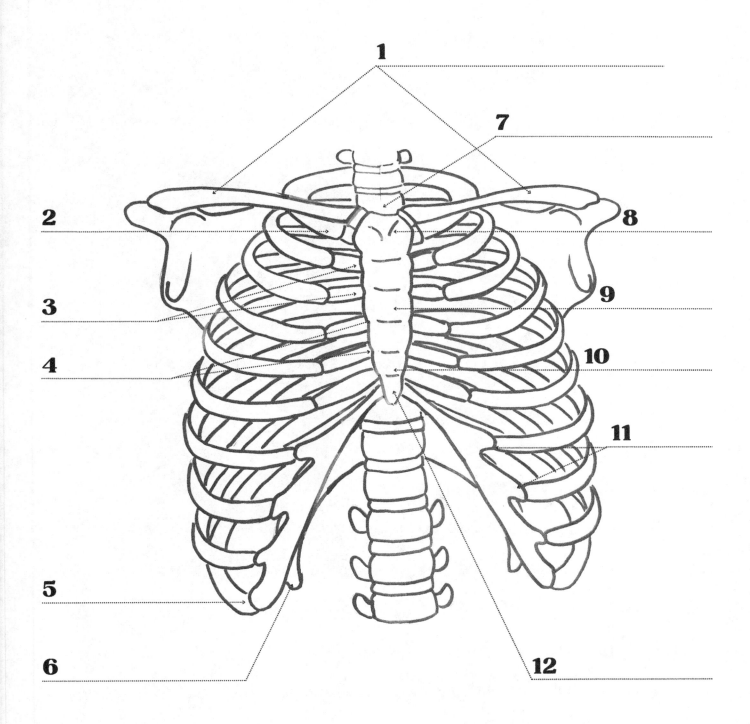

1

2

3

4

5

6

7

8

9

10

11

12

1 - Iliac crest
2 - Ilium
3 - Sacroiliac joint
4 - Sacrum
5 - Anterior superior iliac spine
6 - Pubic bone
7 - Acetabulum
8 - Coccyx
9 - Obturator foramen
10 - Ischium
11 - Coxal bone
12 - Iliac fossa
13 - Ischial spine
14 - Pubic crest
15 - Pubic symphysis
16 - Pubic arch
17 - Posterior superior iliac spine
18 - Greater sciatic notch
19 - Ischial tuberosity
20 - Femur
21 - Anterior inferior iliac spine
22 - Pubic tubercle

Pelvis

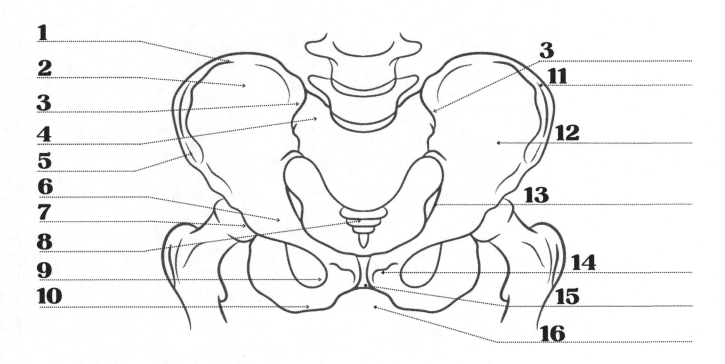

1
2
3
4
5
6
7
8
9
10

3
11
12
13
14
15
16

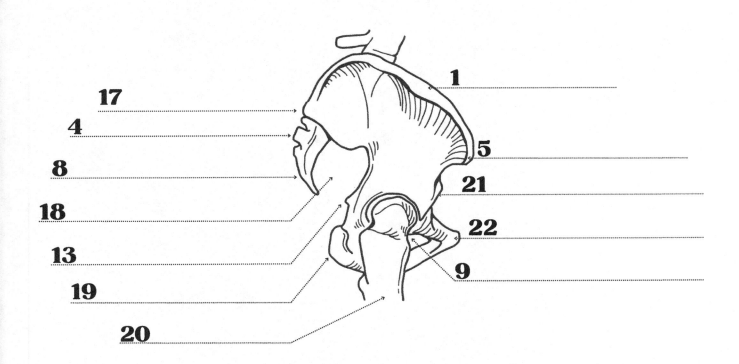

17
4
8
18
13
19
20

1
5
21
22
9

1 - Femur

2 - Lateral collateral ligament

3 - Cruciate ligament

4 - Lateral meniscus

5 - Fibula

6 - Tibia

7 - Patellar ligament

8 - Patella

9 - Medial collateral ligament

10 - Medial meniscus

Knee joint

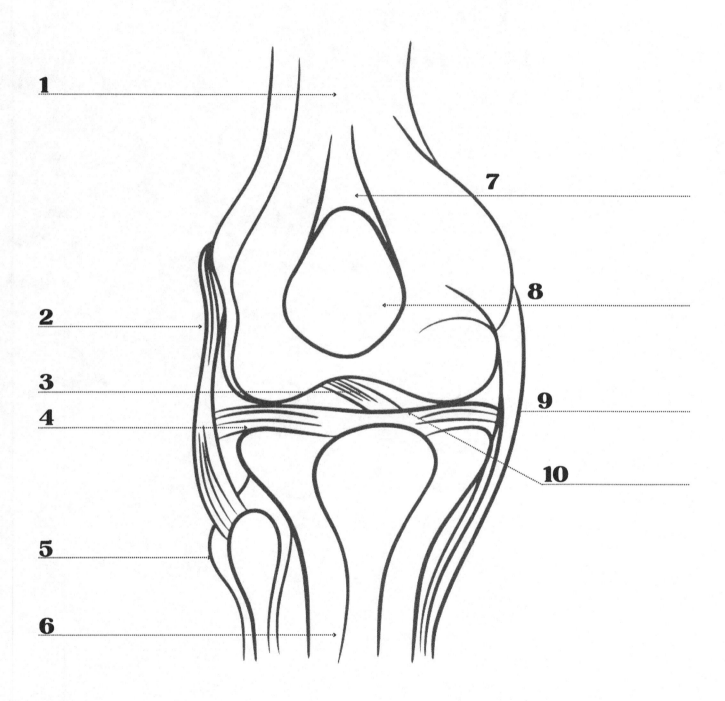

1

2

3

4

5

6

7

8

9

10

Satisfaction Rating Scale
☹ ☹ 😐 🙂 😊

Page Revision Tracker
☐ ☐ ☐ ☐ ☐

1 - Clavicle

2 - Scapula

3 - Acromioclavicular joint

4 - Joint of humerus

5 - Humerus

6 - Humeroradial joint

7 - Humeroulnar joint

8 - Radius

9 - Ulna

10 - Radioulnar joint

11 - Radiocarpal joint

Arm and forearm

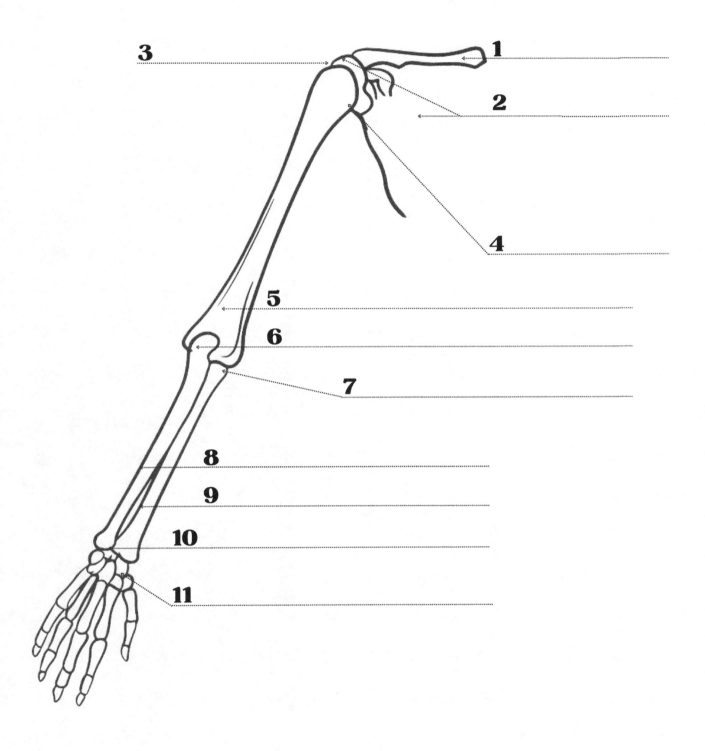

3

1

2

4

5

6

7

8

9

10

11

1 - Pelvis

2 - Sacrum

3 - Femur

4 - Patella

5 - Fibula

6 - Tibia

7 - Tarsal

8 - Metatarsal

9 - Phalanges

Lower limb

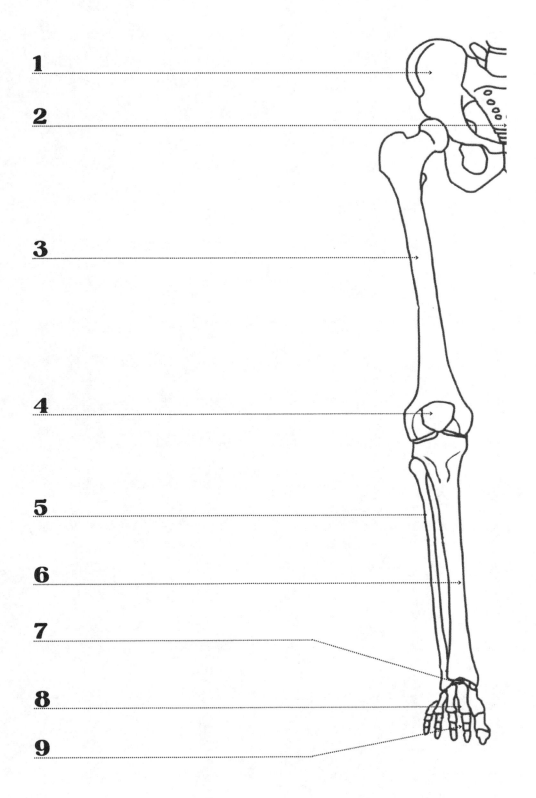

1 ....

2 ....

3 ....

4 ....

5 ....

6 ....

7 ....

8 ....

9 ....

1 - Distal phalanges
2 - Middle palanges
(none on the thumb)
3 - Proximal phalanges
4 - Metacarpals
5 - Carpals - trapezium
6 - Carpals - trapezoid
7 - Carpals - capitate
8 - Carpals - hamate
9 - Carpals - pisiform
10 - Carpals - lunate
11 - Carpals - scaphoid
12 - Carpals - triquentral
13 - Radius
14 - Ulna

Hand

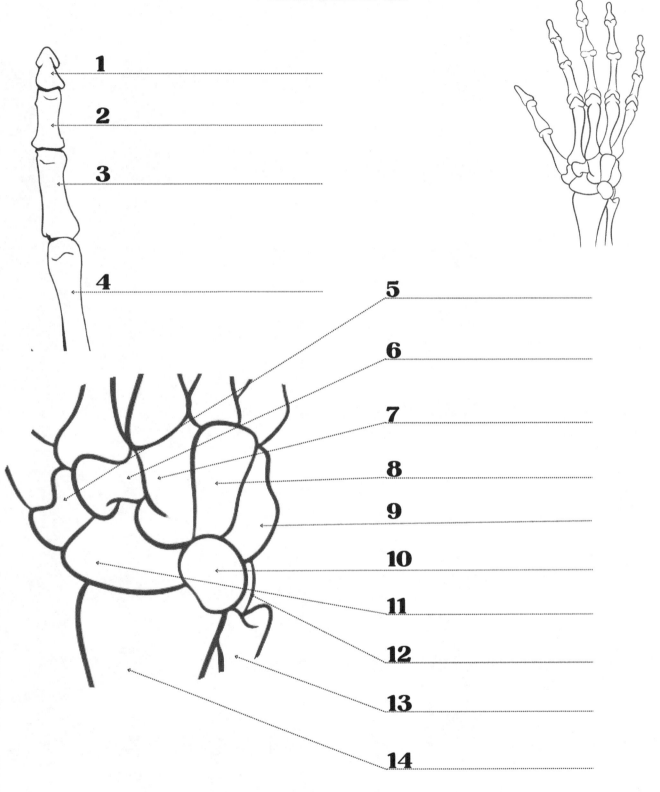

1
2
3
4
5
6
7
8
9
10
11
12
13
14

1 - Tibia
2 - Distal phalanges
3 - Medial phalanges
(none on the big toe)
4 - Proximal phalanges
5 - Metatarsals
6 - Tarsals - cuniform 1
7 - Tarsals - cuniform 2
8 - Tarsals - cuniform 3
9 - Tarsals - cuboid
10 - Tarsals - navicular
11 - Tarsals - talus
12 - Tarsals - calcaneous

Foot

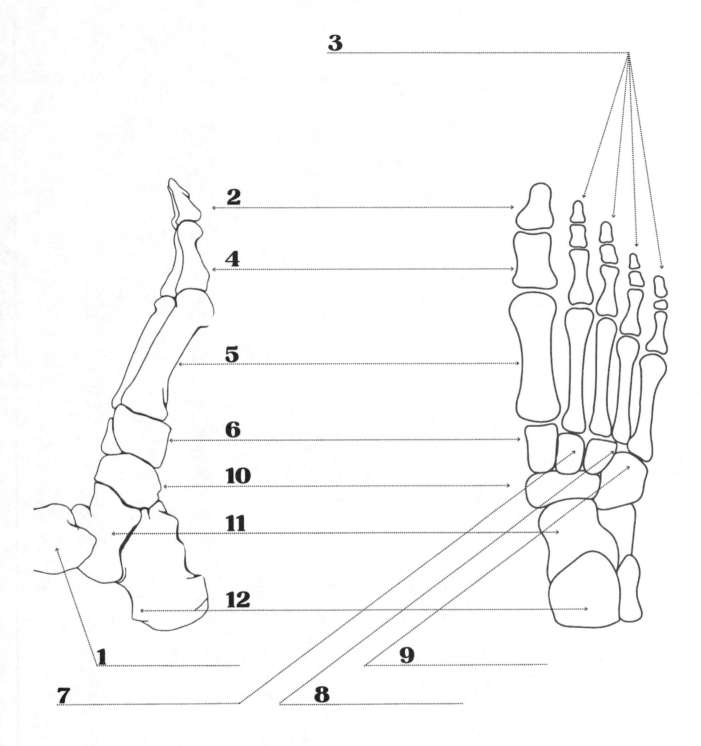

Satisfaction Rating Scale
☹ ☹ 😐 🙂 😊

Page Revision Tracker
☐ ☐ ☐ ☐ ☐

1 - **Intertubercular groove**
2 - **Deltoid tuberosity**
3 - **Lateral supracondylar ridge**
4 - **Lateral epicondyle**
5 - **Medial epicondyle**
6 - **Proximal radioulnar joint**
7 - **Radial tuberosity**
8 - **Styloid process of radius**
9 - **Styloid process of ulna**
10 - **Distal radioulnar joint**

11 - **Head**
12 - **Trochlea**
13 - **Neck**
14 - **Radius**
15 - **Ulna**
16 - **Capitulum**
17 - **Radial fossa**
18 - **Radial notch**
19 - **Ulnar notch**
20 - **Head of ulna**
21 - **Anatomic neck**

22 - **Greater tubercle**
23 - **Lesser tubercle**
24 - **Humerus**
25 - **Coronoid process**
26 - **Surgical neck**
27 - **Coronoid fossa**
28 - **Trochlear notch**
29 - **Olecranon process**

Humerus, radius and ulna

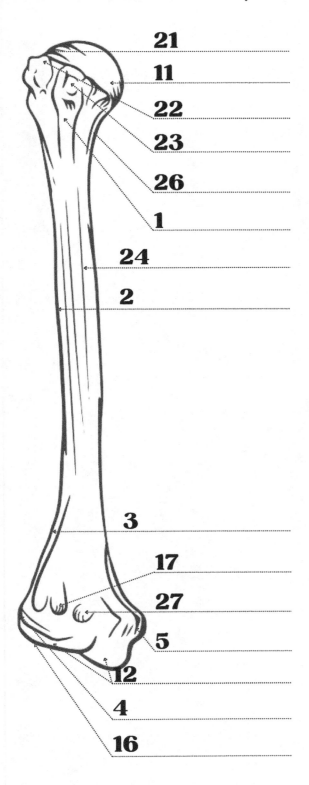

21
11
22
23
26
1
24
2
3
17
27
5
12
4
16

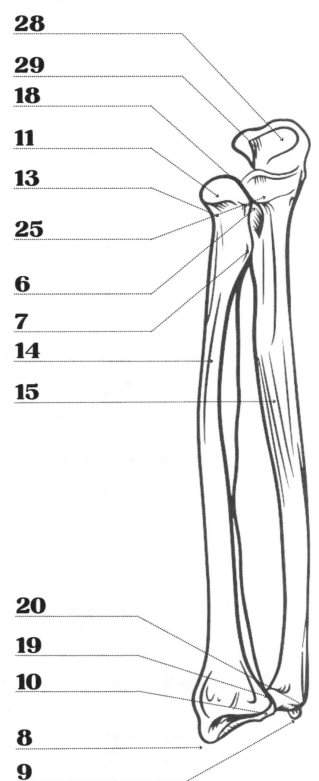

28
29
18
11
13
25
6
7
14
15
20
19
10
8
9

1 - Lateral condyle

2 - Head

3 - Intercondylar eminence

4 - Medial condyle

5 - Articular surface of medial condyle

6 - Articular surface of lateral condyle

7 - Tibial tuberosity

8 - Fibula

9 - Tibia

10 - Lateral malleolus

11 - Medial malleolus

12 - Articular surface of medial malleolus

Tibia and fibula

6 ....

5 ....

3 ....

1 ....

4 ....

7 ....

2 ....

8 ....

9 ....

11 ....

12 ....

10 ....

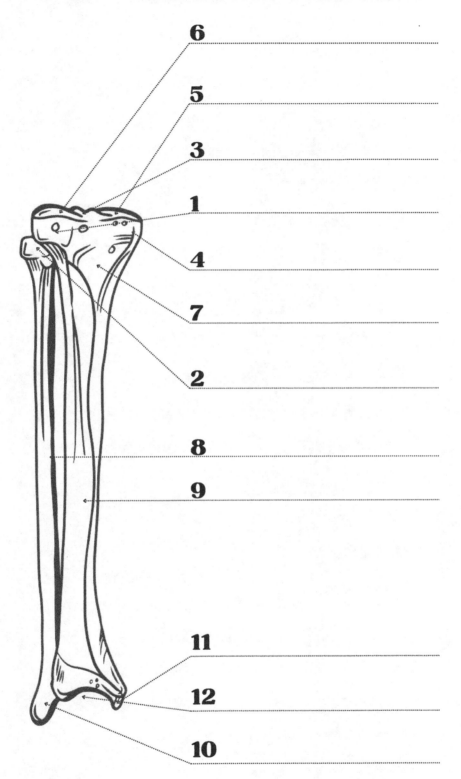

1 - Deltoid

2 - Pectoralis major

3 - Rectus abdominis

4 - Abdominal external oblique

5 - Iliopsoas

6 - Quadriceps femoris

7 - Peroneus longus

8 - Peroneus brevis

9 - Rotator cuff

10 - Biceps brachii

11 - Brachialis

12 - Pronator teres

13 - Brachioradialis

14 - Adductor muscles

15 - Tibialis anterior

The muscles of the human body

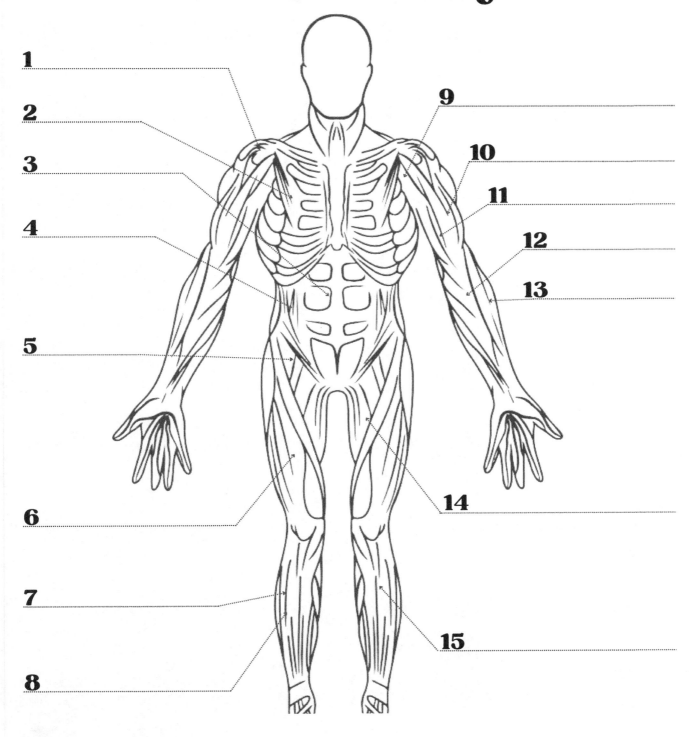

1

2

3

4

5

6

7

8

9

10

11

12

13

14

15

1 - Frontalis

2 - Orbicularis oris

3 - Orbicularis oculi

4 - Temporalis

5 - Lavator labii superioris

6 - Zygomaticus minor

7 - Zygomaticus major

8 - Risorius

9 - Depressor anguli oris

10 - Depressor labii inferioris

11 - Mentalis

12 - Platysma

13 - Masseter

14 - Buccinator

The muscles of the face

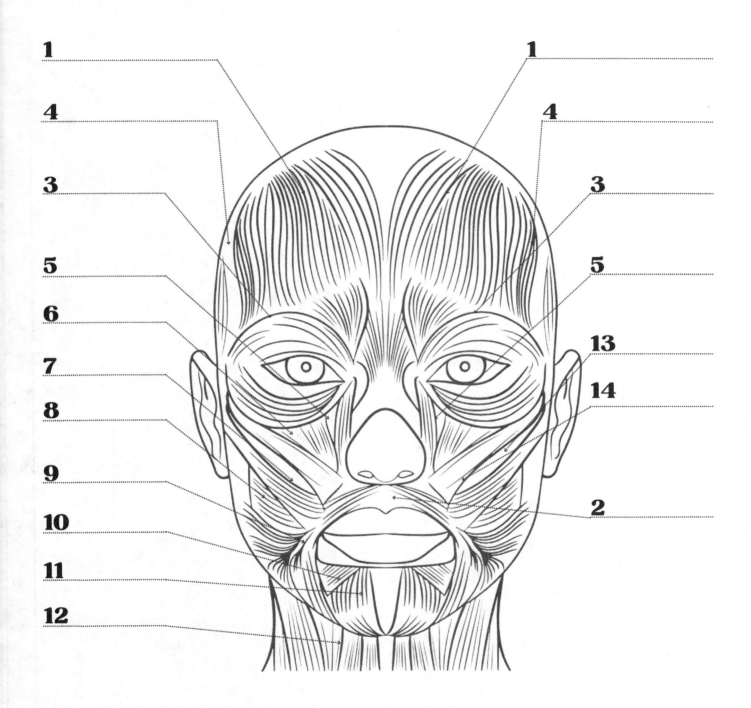

1

4

3

5

6

7

8

9

10

11

12

1

4

3

5

13

14

2

1 - **Trapezius**

2 - **Deltoid**

3 - **Latissimus dorsi**

4 - **Levator scapulae**

5 - **Rhombold minor**

6 - **Rhombold major**

7 - **Clavicle**

8 - **Supraspinatus**

9 - **Infraspinatus**

10 - **Teres minor**

11 - **Teres major**

Muscles of the posterior neck, schoulders and thorax

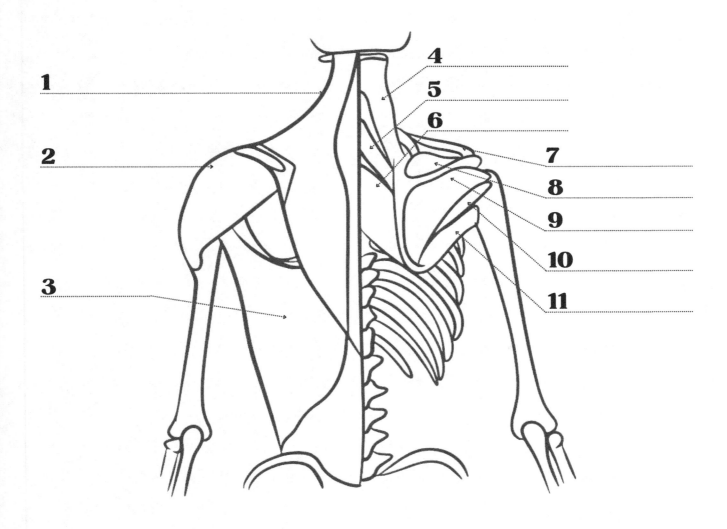

1

2

3

4

5

6

7

8

9

10

11

1 - **Platysma**

2 - **Sternocleidomastoid**

3 - **Trapezius**

4 - **Deltoid**

5 - **Biceps brachii**

6 - **Serratus anterior**

7 - **Pectoralis major**

8 - **Pectoralis minor**

9 - **Carocobrachialis**

10 - **Subscapularis**

11 - **Exsternal oblique**

12 - **Internal oblique**

13 - **Transversus abdominus**

14 - **Rectus abdominus**

Muscles of the anterior neck, schoulders and thorax

1
4
7
5
6
11
13
12

3
2
10
9
8
14

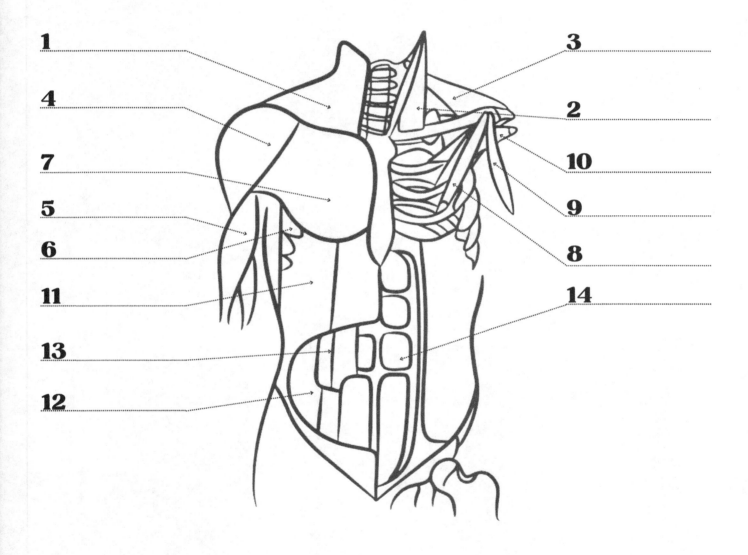

1 - Deltoid
2 - Biceps brachii
3 - Triceps brachii
4 - Brachialis
5 - Brachioradialis
6 - Pronator teres
7 - Flexor carpi radialis
8 - Palmaris longus
9 - Flexor carpi ulnaris

Muscles of the anterior arm and forearm

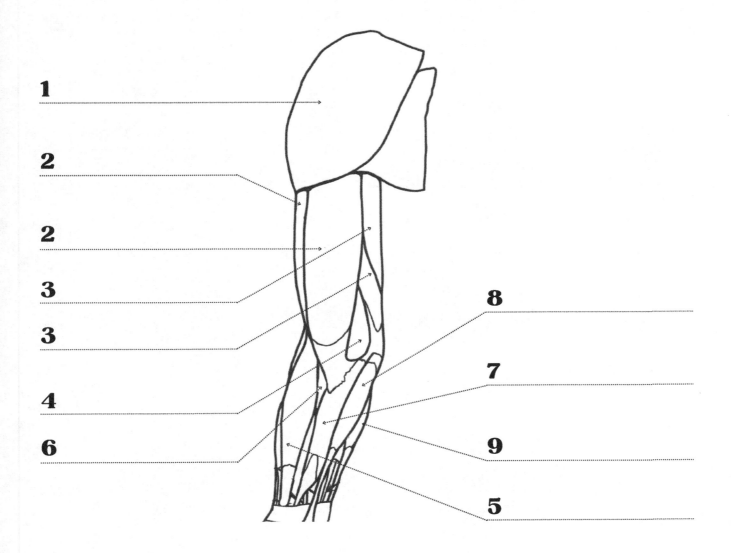

1

2

2

3

3

4

6

8

7

9

5

1 - Triceps brachii

2 - Anconeus

3 - Extensor carpi ulnaris

4 - Flexor carpi ulnaris

5 - Extensor digiti minimi

6 - Deltoid

7 - Brachialis

8 - Brachioradialis

9 - Extensor carpi radialis longus

10 - Extensor carpi radialis brevis

11 - Extensor digitorum

12 - Abductor pollicis longus

13 - Extensor pollicis brevis

14 - Extensor pollicis longus

Muscles of the posterior arm and forearm

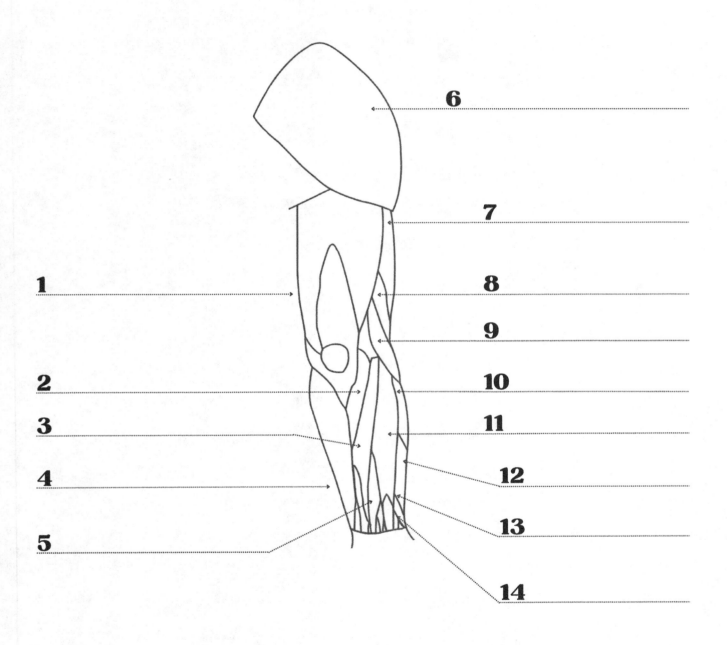

1
2
3
4
5

6
7
8
9
10
11
12
13
14

1 - **Tensor fasciae lata**

2 - **Rectus femoris**

3 - **Vastus lateralis**

4 - **Iliopsoas**

5 - **Inguinal ligament**

6 - **Pectineus**

7 - **Adductor longus**

8 - **Gracilus**

9 - **Adductor magnus**

10 - **Sartorius**

11 - **Vastus medialis**

12 - **Patella**

Muscles of the anterior thigh

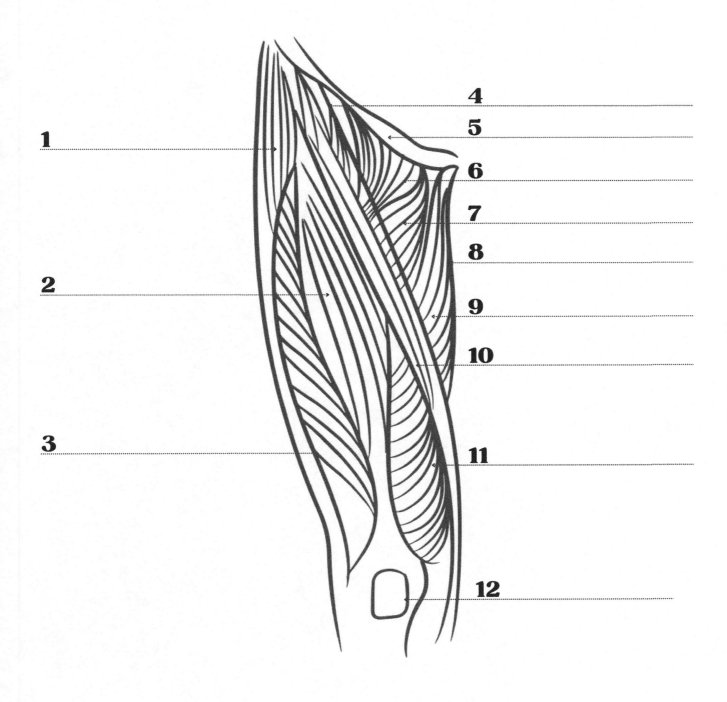

1

2

3

4

5

6

7

8

9

10

11

12

1 - Gluteus maximus
2 - Gracilis
3 - Adductor magnus
4 - Semitendinosus
5 - Semimembranosus
6 - Gluteus medius
7 - Iliotibial tract
8 - Biceps femoris: long head
9 - Biceps femoris: short head

Muscles of the posterior thigh

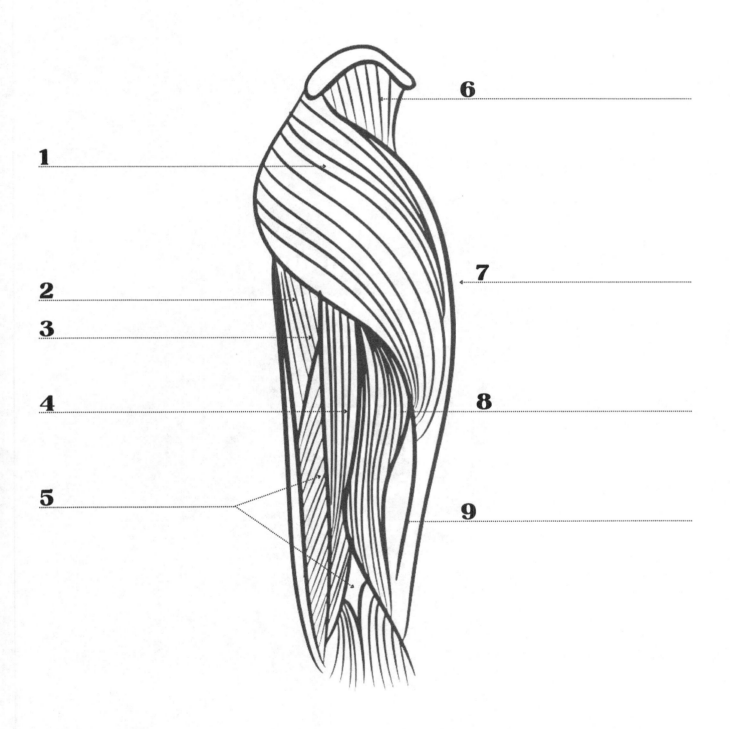

1 ....

2 ....

3 ....

4 ....

5 ....

6 ....

7 ....

8 ....

9 ....

1 - Head of the fibula

2 - Gastrocnemius

3 - Soleus

4 - Peroneus longus

5 - Peroneus brevis

6 - Flexor hallicus longus

7 - Peroneal retinaculum

8 - Lateral malleolus

9 - Patella

10 - Extensor digitorum longus

11 - Tibialis anterior

12 - Tensor hallicus longus

13 - Peroneus tertius

14 - Superior extensor retinaculum

15 - Inferior extensor retinaculum

Muscles of the leg and foot

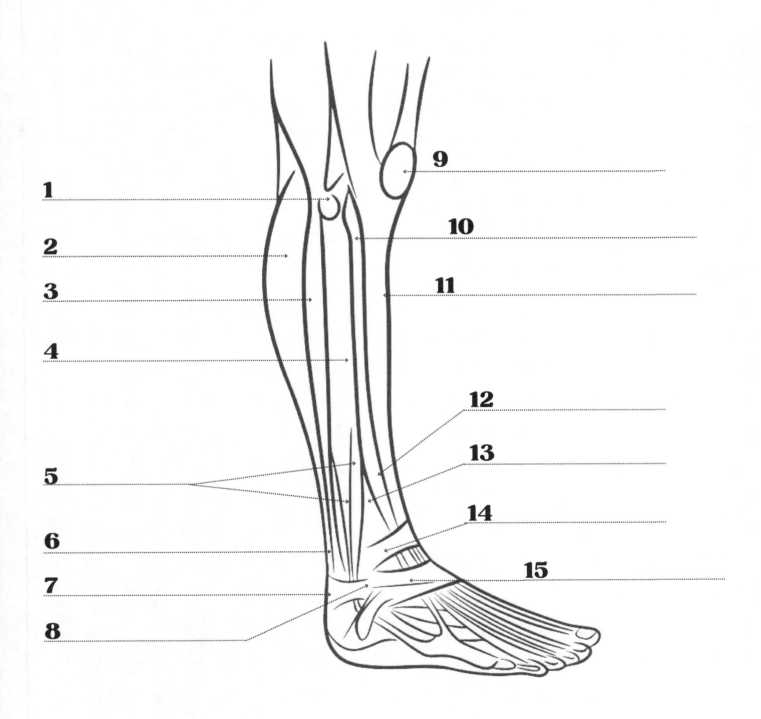

1

2

3

4

5

6

7

8

9

10

11

12

13

14

15

1 - **Jugular veins**

2 - **Carotid arteries**

3 - **Superior vena cava**

4 - **Aorta**

5 - **Pulmonary arteries**

6 - **Heart**

7 - **Lungs**

8 - **Stomach**

9 - **Diaphragm**

10 - **Kidneys**

11 - **Liver**

12 - **Femoral artery**

13 - **Femoral vein**

Circulatory system

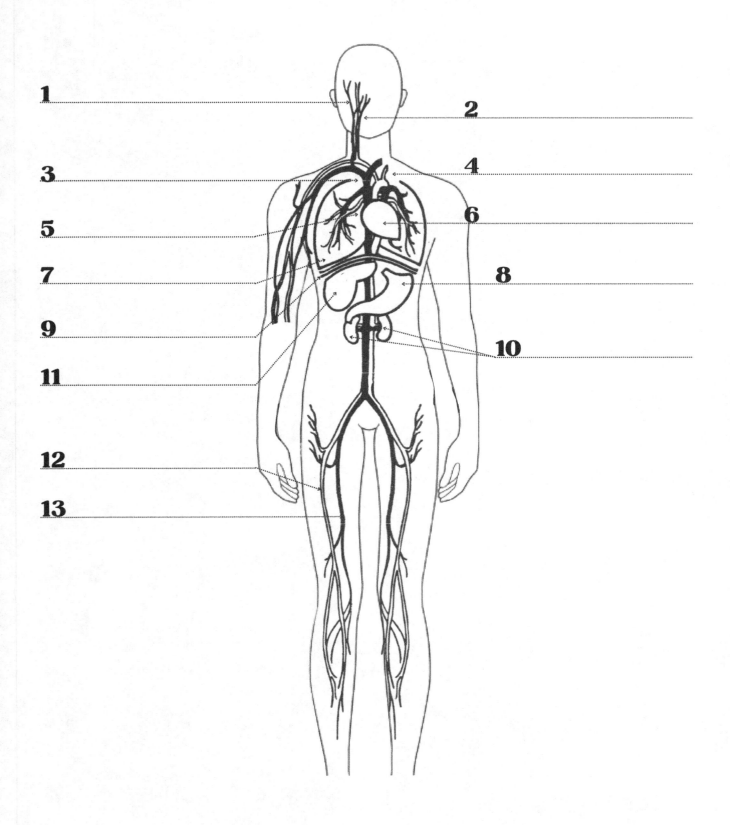

1

2

3

4

5

6

7

8

9

10

11

12

13

1 - **Tunica interna**
2 - **Elastin layer**
3 - **Tunica media**
4 - **Tunica externa**
5 - **Serosa**

Anatomy of the artery

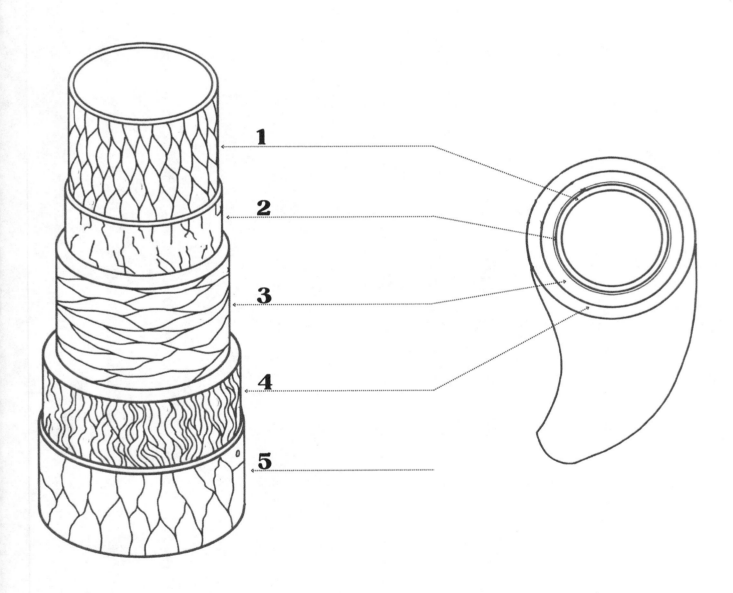

1

2

3

4

5

1 - Left subclavian artery
2 - Left common carotid artery
3 - Right subclavian artery
4 - Superior vena cava
5 - Right pulmonary arterie
6 - Aortic arch
7 - Right pulmonary veins
8 - Right atrium
9 - Right coronary artery
10 - Marginal artery
11 - Right ventricle
12 - Inferior vena cava
13 - Cardial muscle
14 - Left pulmonary artery
15 - Left pulmonary veins
16 - Left atrium
17 - Circumflex artery
18 - Anterior inter-ventricular artery
19 - Left ventricle
20 - Apex of heart
21 - Descending aorta

Anatomy of the heart

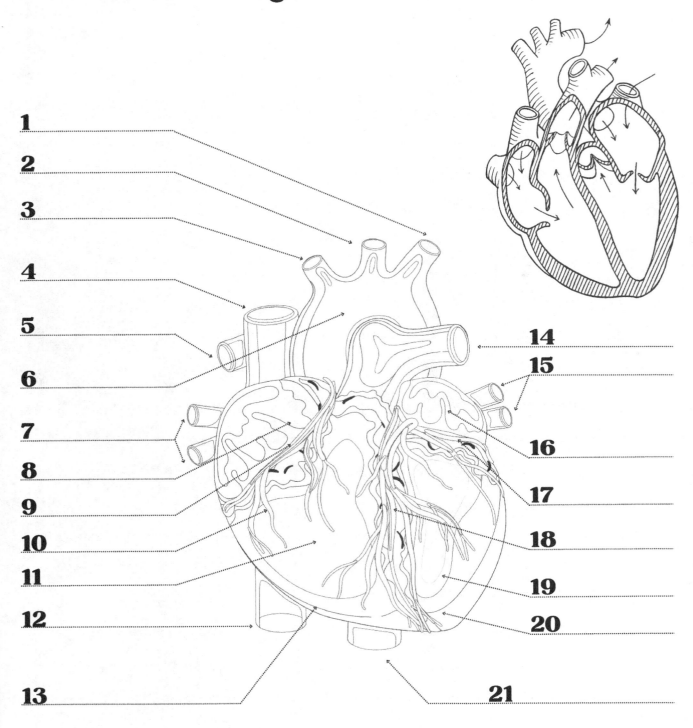

1 ....

2 ....

3 ....

4 ....

5 ....

6 ....

7 ....

8 ....

9 ....

10 ....

11 ....

12 ....

13 ....

14 ....

15 ....

16 ....

17 ....

18 ....

19 ....

20 ....

21 ....

1 - Trachea

2 - Right pulmonary artery

3 - Lobar arteries

4 - Right pulmonary veins

5 - Right lung (3 lobes)

6 - Left pulmonary artery

7 - Lobar arteries

8 - Left pulmonary veins

9 - Left lung (2 lobes)

10 - Alveoli

11 - Pulmonary capillary

Pulmonary circulation

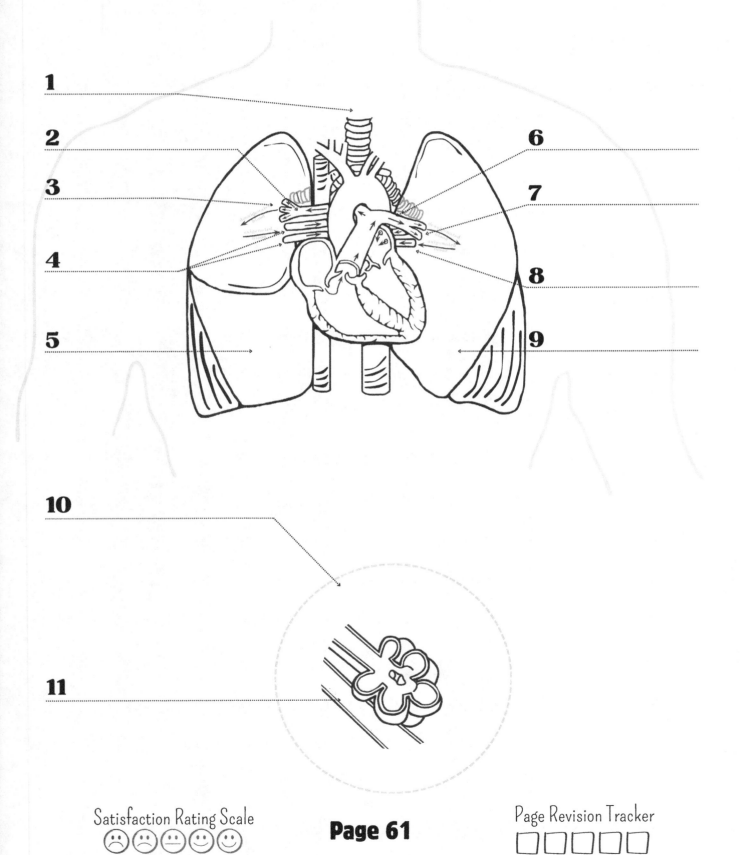

1

2

3

4

5

6

7

8

9

10

11

1 - Inferior phrenic
2 - Celiac trunk
3 - Suprarenals
4 - Superior mesenteric
5 - Renals
6 - Gonadals
7 - Inferior mesenteric
8 - Lumbar arteries
9 - Common iliac artery
10 - Internal iliac artery
11 - Vertebral artery
12 - Common carotid artery
13 - Subclavian artery
14 - Axillary artery
15 - Coronaries arteries
16 - Brachial artery
17 - Radial artery
18 - Ulnar artery
19 - Digital arteries
20 - External iliac artery
21 - Median sacral artery
22 - Deep femoral artery
23 - Femoral artery
24 - Popliteal artery
25 - Anterior tibial artery
26 - Posterior tibial artery
27 - Arcuate artery

Arteries of the circulatory system

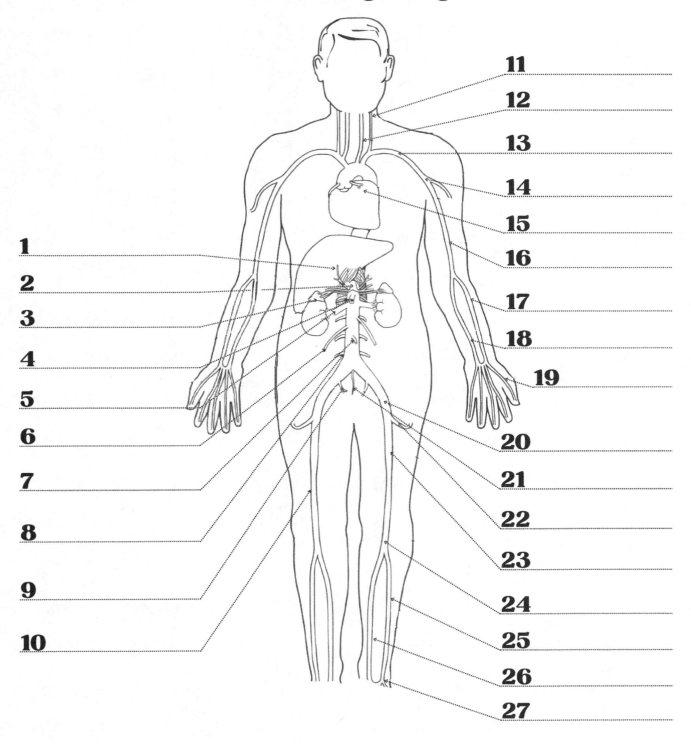

11 ....

12 ....

13 ....

14 ....

15 ....

16 ....

17 ....

18 ....

19 ....

1 ....

2 ....

3 ....

4 ....

5 ....

6 ....

7 ....

8 ....

9 ....

10 ....

20 ....

21 ....

22 ....

23 ....

24 ....

25 ....

26 ....

27 ....

1 - Occipital artery
2 - Internal carotid artery
3 - External carotid artery
4 - Vertebral artery
5 - Subclavian artery
6 - Superficial temporal artery
7 - Ophthalmic artery
8 - Maxillary artery
9 - Facial artery
10 - Lingual artery
11 - Superior thyroid artery
12 - Larynx
13 - Thyroid gland
14 - Common carotid artery
15 - Clavicle
16 - Brachiocephalic trunk
17 - Aortic arch

Arteries of the head and neck

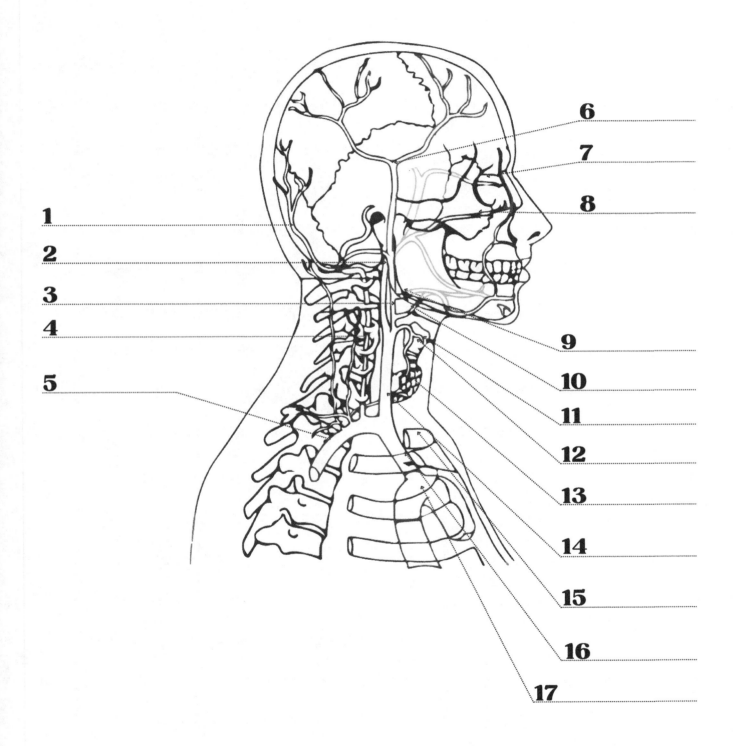

1

2

3

4

5

6

7

8

9

10

11

12

13

14

15

16

17

1 - **Subsclavian artery**

2 - **Axillary artery**

3 - **Thoracoacromial trunk**

4 - **Lateral thoracic artery**

5 - **Subscapular artery**

6 - **Posterior humeral circumflex artery**

7 - **Anterior humeral circumflex artery**

8 - **Brachial artery**

9 - **Deep brachial artery**

10 - **Common interosseous artery**

11 - **Radial artery**

12 - **Ulnar artery**

13 - **Deep palmar arch**

14 - **Superficial palmar arch**

15 - **Digital arteries**

Arteries of the upper limb

1 ....

2 ....

3 ....

4 ....

5 ....

6 ....

7 ....

8 ....

9 ....

10 ....

11 ....

12 ....

13 ....

14 ....

15 ....

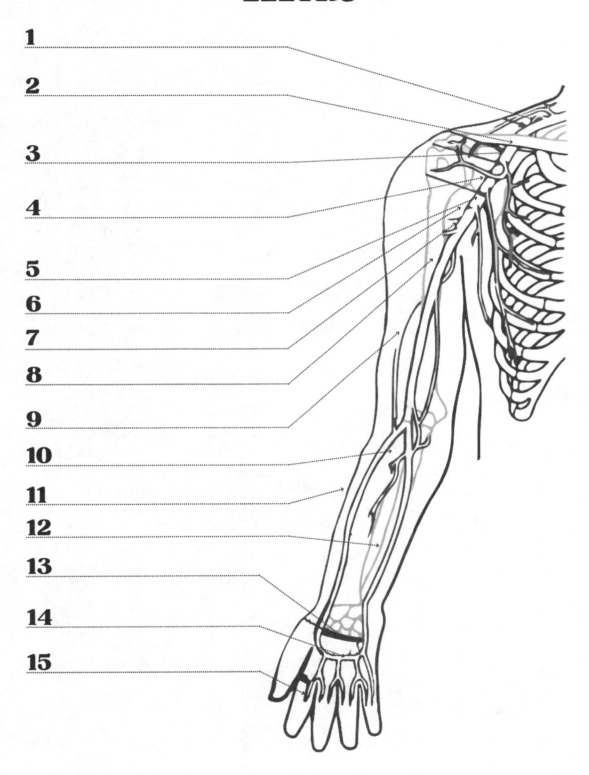

1 - Common iliac artery

2 - Internal iliac artery

3 - External iliac artery

4 - Femoral artery

5 - Deep femoral artery

6 - Lateral circumflex artery

7 - Medial circumflex artery

8 - Popliteal artery

9 - Anterior tibial artery

10 - Posterior tibial artery

11 - Peroneal artery

12 - Dorsalis pedis artery

13 - Arcuate artery

14 - Metatarsal artery

15 - Plantar arch

Arteries of the pelvis and lower limb

1

2

3

4

5

6

7

8

9

10

11

12

13

14

15

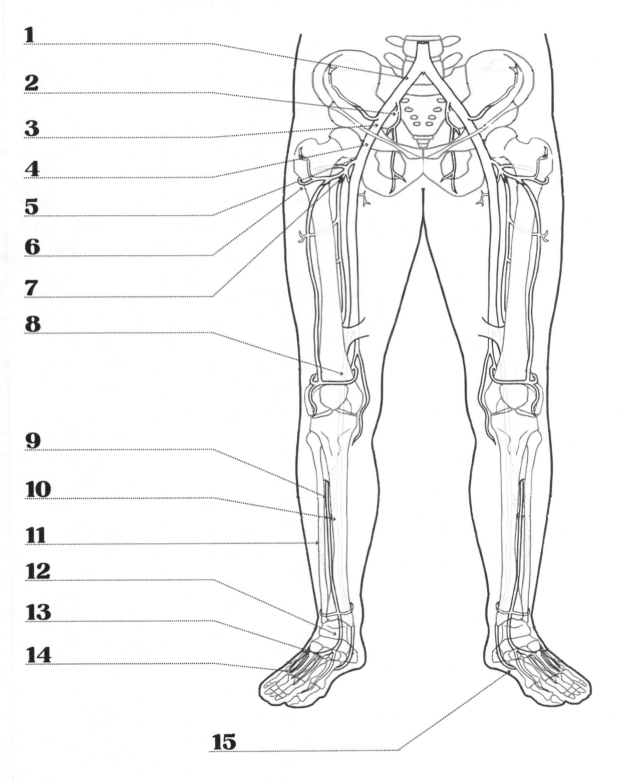

1 - Right inferior phrenic
2 - Common hepatic artery
3 - Right suprarenal artery
4 - Right renal artery
5 - Right lumbar arteries
6 - Right gonadal artery
7 - Right common iliac artery
8 - Diaphragm
9 - Left inferior phrenic
10 - Celiac trunk
11 - Splenic artery
12 - Left gastric artery
13 - Left suprarenal artery
14 - Superior mesenteric
15 - Left renal artery
16 - Left lumbar arteries
17 - Left gonadal artery
18 - Inferior mesenteric
19 - Left common iliac artery
20 - Median sacral artery

Blood vessels of
abdominal aorta

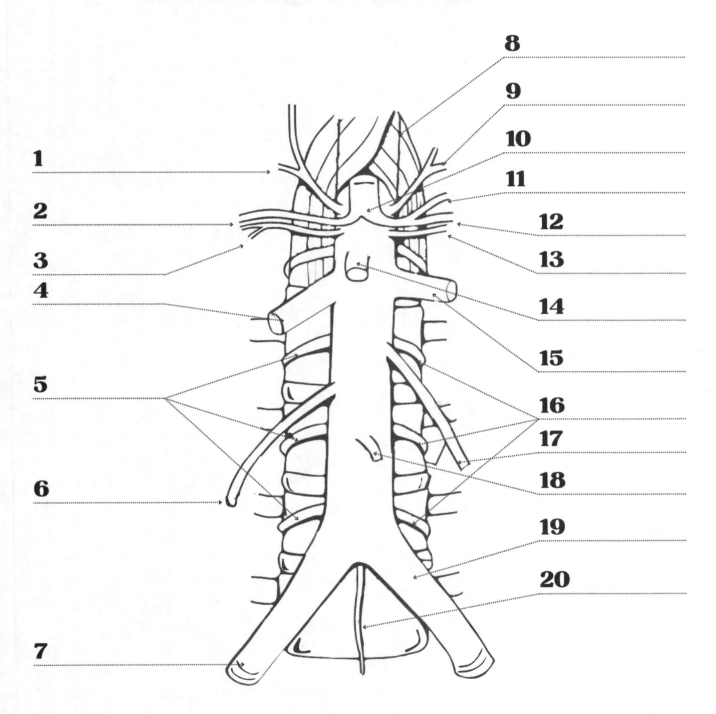

1
2
3
4
5
6
7

8
9
10
11
12
13
14
15
16
17
18
19
20

Satisfaction Rating Scale

Page Revision Tracker

1 - Liver

2 - Gallbladder

3 - Duodenum

4 - Duodena jejunal junction

5 - Ascending colon

6 - Cecum

7 - Appendix

8 - Ileum

9 - Salivary glands

10 - Esophagus

11 - Stomach

12 - Pancreas

13 - Left colic flexure

14 - Transverse colon

15 - Jejunum

16 - Descending colon

17 - Sigmoid colon

18 - Rectum

19 - Anus

Organic of the digestive tract

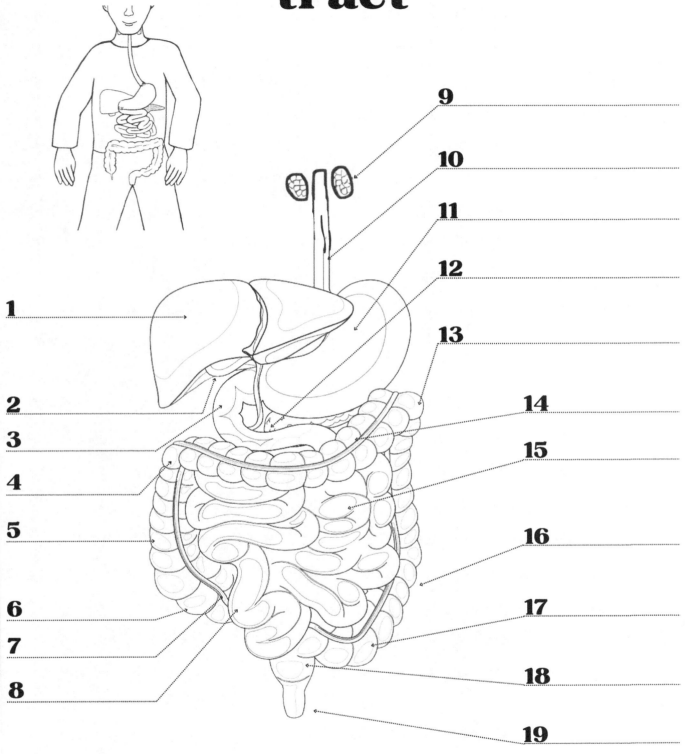

1 _____

2 _____

3 _____

4 _____

5 _____

6 _____

7 _____

8 _____

9 _____

10 _____

11 _____

12 _____

13 _____

14 _____

15 _____

16 _____

17 _____

18 _____

19 _____

1 - Nasal cavity

2 - Oral cavity

3 - Mandible

4 - Larynx

5 - Trachea

6 - Opening for eustacian tube

7 - Nasopharynx

8 - Uvula

9 - Oropharynx

10 - Epiglottis

11 - Laryngopharynx

12 - Esophogus

Mouth, pharynx and esophagus

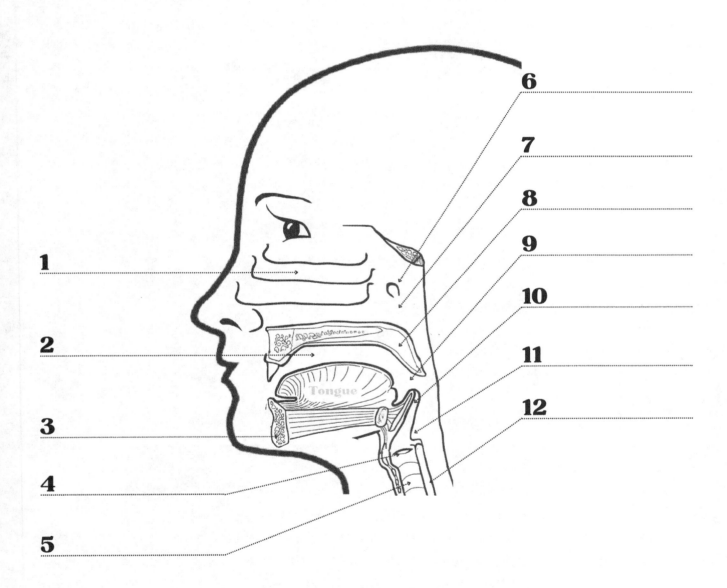

Tongue

1

2

3

4

5

6

7

8

9

10

11

12

1 - Interior vena cava
2 - Common iliac veins
3 - Rectum
4 - Anal crypt
5 - Dentate line
6 - External iliac vein
7 - Internal iliac vein
8 - Internal rectal vein
9 - Middle rectail vein
10 - Internal rectal venous plexus
11 - External rectal venous plexus

Rectum anatomy

1

2

3

6

7

8

9

4

10

5

11

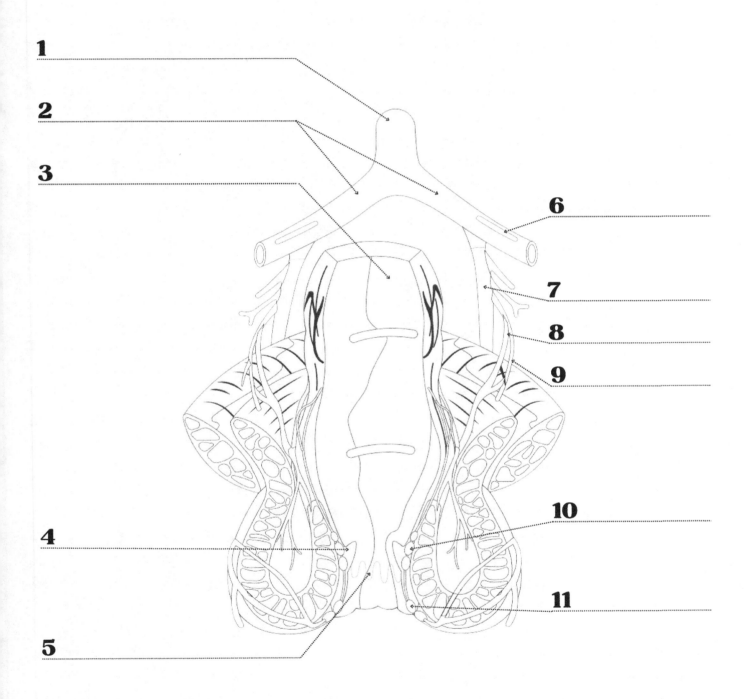

1 - Liver
2 - Common hepatic duct
3 - Cystic duct
4 - Common bile duct
5 - Stomach
6 - Common bile duct
7 - Pancreas
8 - Duodenum

Liver and stomach

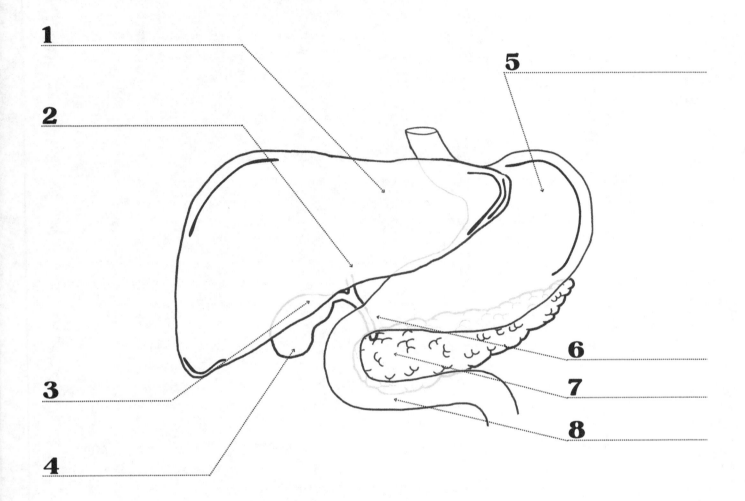

1

2

3

4

5

6

7

8

1 - Duodenum

2 - Right colic

3 - Ascending colon

4 - Ileum

5 - Cecum

6 - Appendix

7 - Transverse colon

8 - Left colic

9 - Jejunum

10 - Descending colon

11 - Sigmoid colon

12 - Rectum

13 - Anus

Structure of the intestines

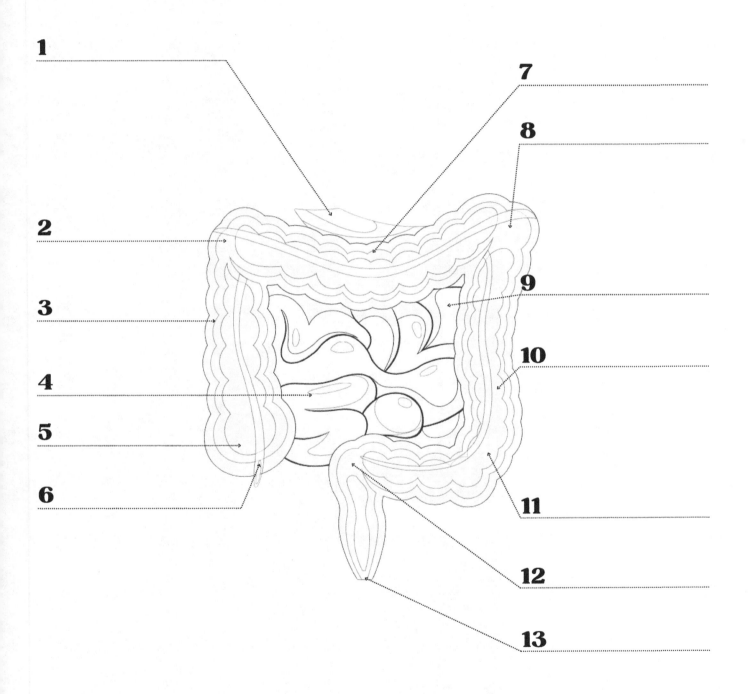

1

2

3

4

5

6

7

8

9

10

11

12

13

Satisfaction Rating Scale

Page Revision Tracker

1 - Nostril
2 - Mouth
3 - Trachea
4 - Primary bronchus
5 - Secondary bronchus
6 - Tertiary bronchus
7 - Bronchioles
8 - Lungs
9 - Diaphragm
10 - Alveoli
11 - Capillary

Respiratory system

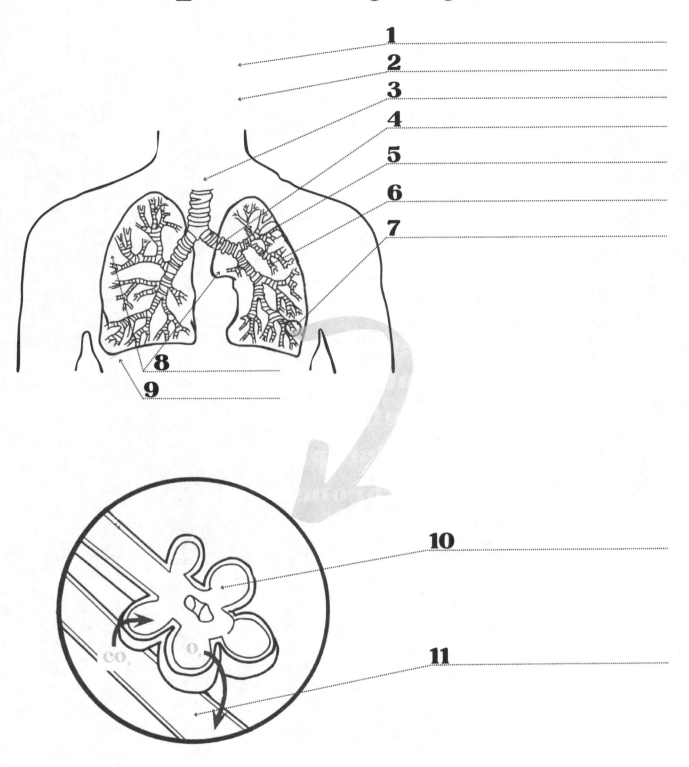

1 ....

2 ....

3 ....

4 ....

5 ....

6 ....

7 ....

10 ....

11 ....

1 - Trachea
2 - Bronchi
3 - Lungs
4 - Diaphragm
5 - Parietal pleura
6 - Visceral pleura
7 - Lung bronchioles
8 - Rib section
9 - Intercostal muscle

Respiratory system structures

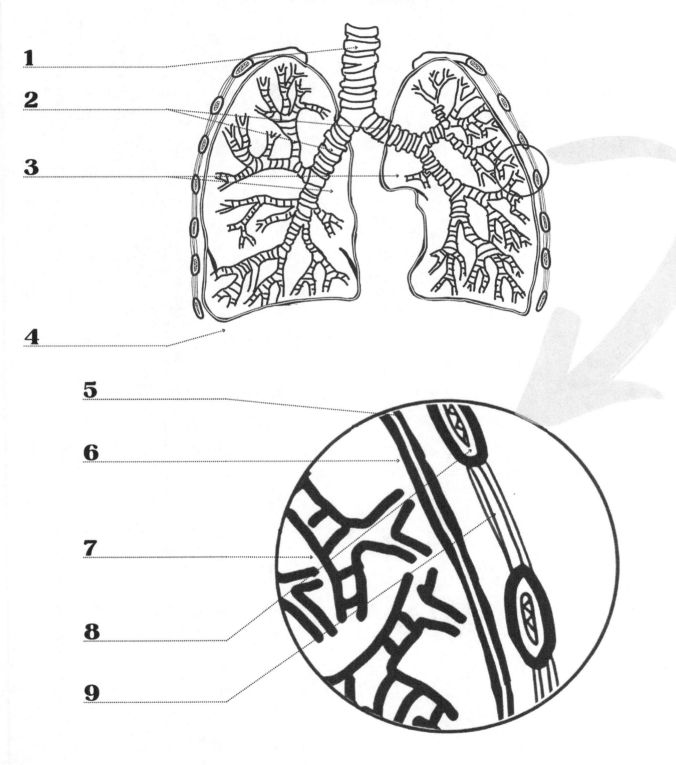

1

2

3

4

5

6

7

8

9

1 - Ganglion
2 - Nerve
3 - Brain
4 - Spinal cord

Nervous system

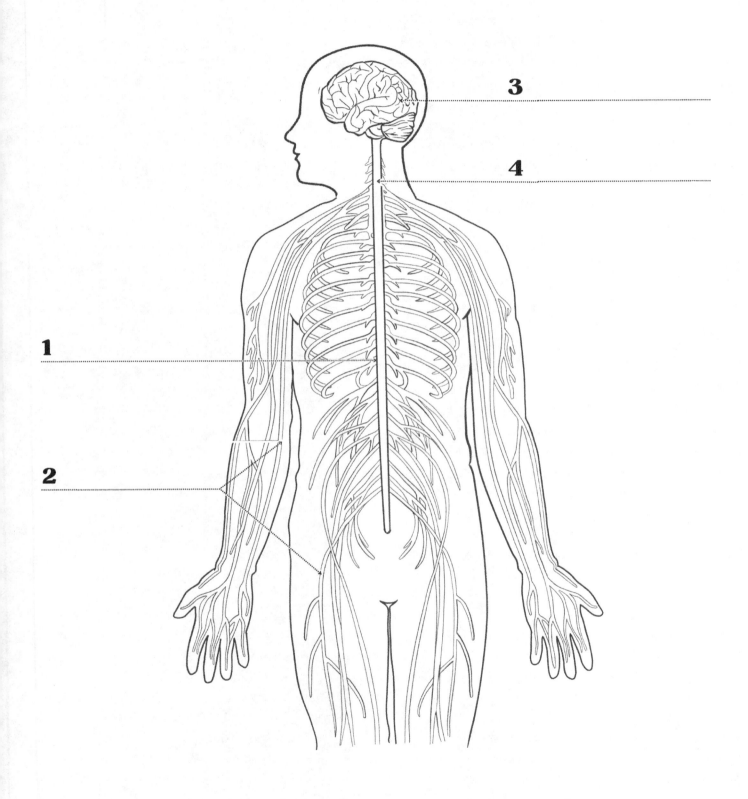

1

2

3

4

1 - **Parietal lobe**
2 - **Occipital lobe**
3 - **Neuron**
4 - **Body**
5 - **Frontal lobe**
6 - **Temporal lobe**
7 - **Dentrites**
8 - **Muscle**

Nerve cell or neurone

1

2

6

7

4

5

8

9

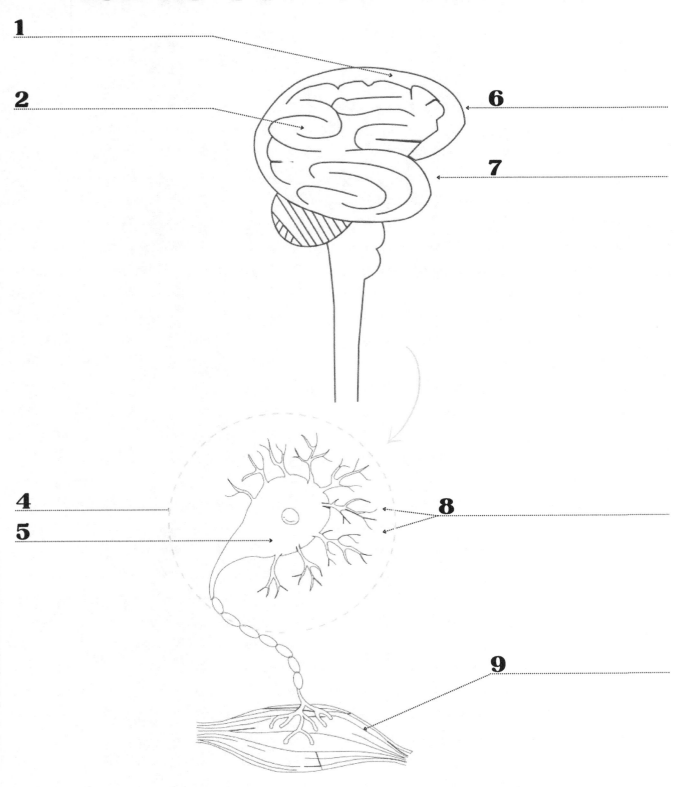

1 - **Olfactory nerve**

2 - **Optic nerve**

3 - **Oculomotor nerve**

4 - **Trochlear nerve**

5 - **Trigeminal nerve**

6 - **Abducens nerve**

7 - **Facial nerve**

8 - **Vestibulococlear nerve**

9 - **Glossopharyngeal nerve**

10 - **Vagus nerve**

11 - **Accessory nerve**

12 - **Hypoglossal nerve**

Cranial nerves

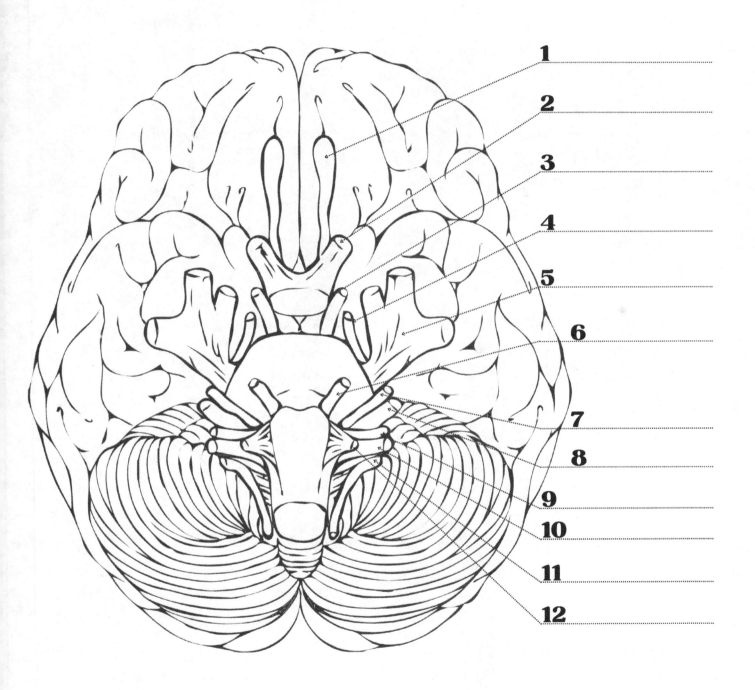

1 ....

2 ....

3 ....

4 ....

5 ....

6 ....

7 ....

8 ....

9 ....

10 ....

11 ....

12 ....

1 - See
2 - Taste
3 - Smell
4 - Hear
5 - Touch

The five senses

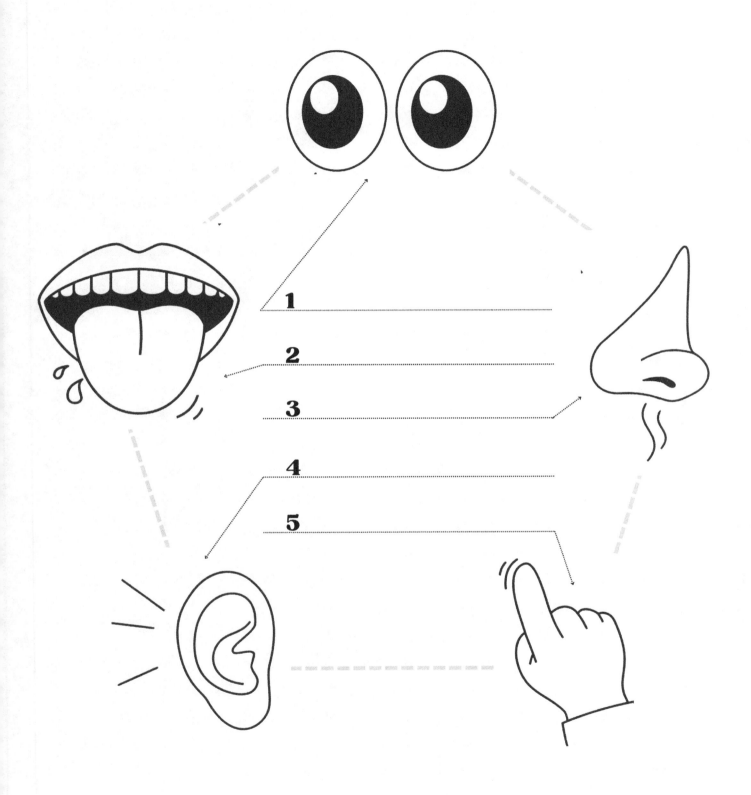

1 _____

2 _____

3 _____

4 _____

5 _____

1- Cornea

2 - Iris

3 - Pupil

4 - Aqueous humor

5 - Lens

6 - Ciliary muscle

7 - Vitreous humor

8 - Sclera

9 - Choroid

10 - Retina

11 - Fovea

12 - Optic nerve

The structures of the eye

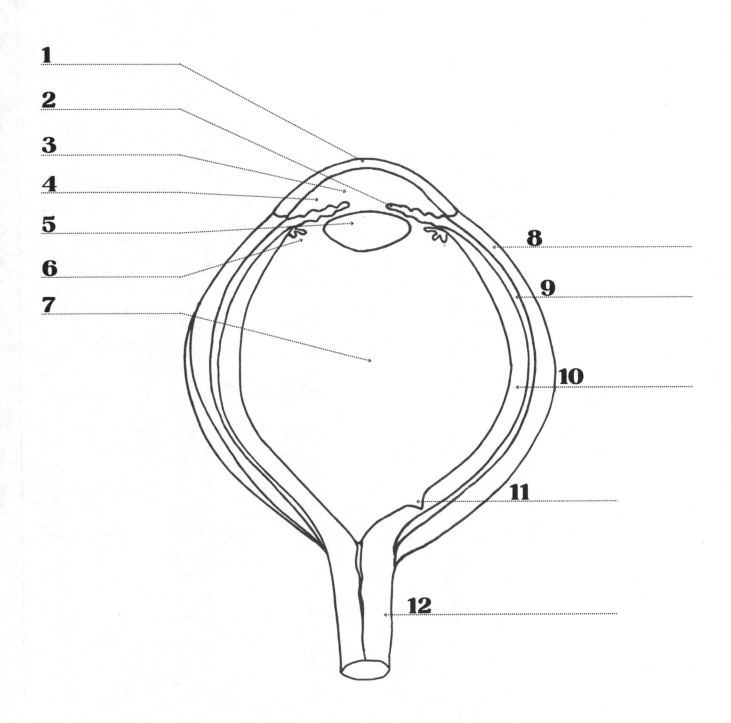

1
2
3
4
5
6
7

8
9
10
11
12

Satisfaction Rating Scale
☹ ☹ 😐 🙂 😊

Page Revision Tracker
☐ ☐ ☐ ☐ ☐

1 - **Olfactory bulb**
2 - **Olfactory receptor cells**
3 - **Nasal conchae**
4 - **Nostril**
5 - **Olfactory nerve**

Sense of smell

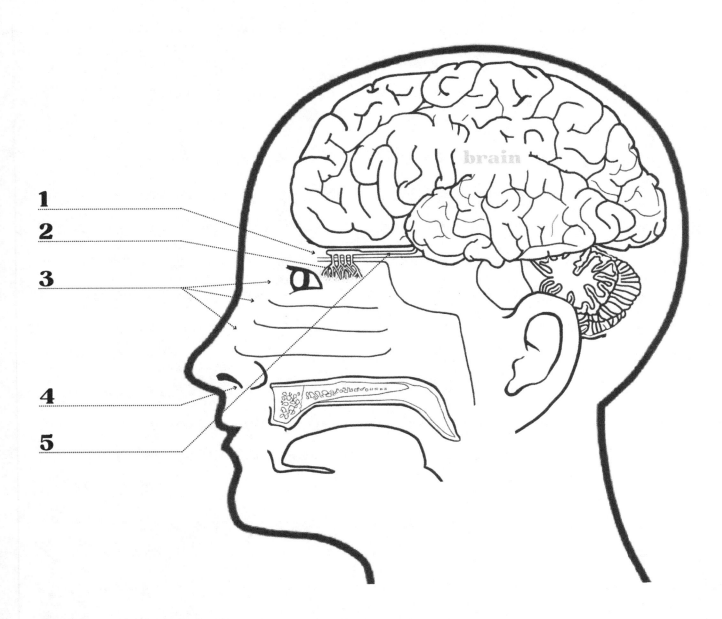

1

2

3

4

5

1 - Hair
2 - Blood capillaries
3 - Nerve fiber
4 - Papilla of hair
5 - Hair follicle
6 - Arrector pili muscle
7 - Pore
8 - Epidermis
9 - Dermis
10 - Hypodermis
11 - Sweat gland
12 - Vein
13 - Artery
14 - Cebaceous gland

Sense organs and other structures of the skin

1

2

3

7

8

9

10

4

5

11

12

13

6

14

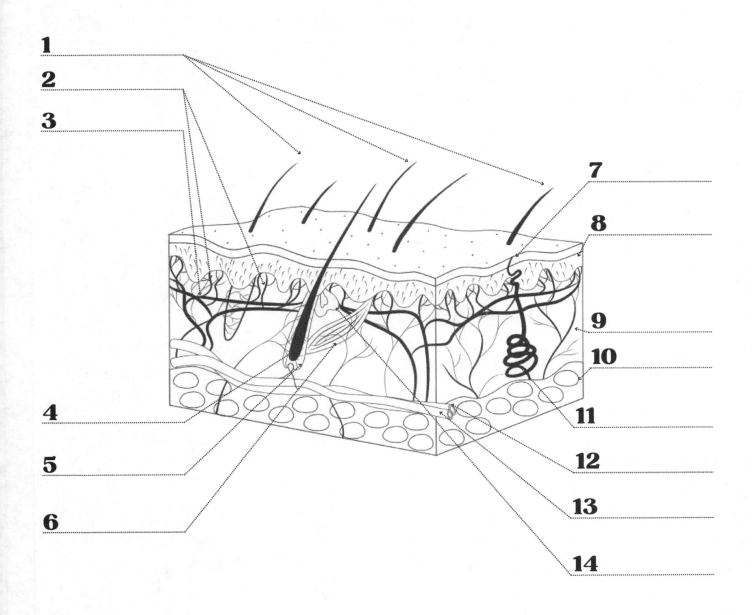

1 - Auricle

2 - Ear canal

3 - Earlobe

4 - Ear drum

5 - Malleus

6 - Incus

7 - Staples

8 - Cochlea

9 - Eustachian tube

10 - Semi-circular canals

11 - Vestibulocochlear nerve

Structures of the ear

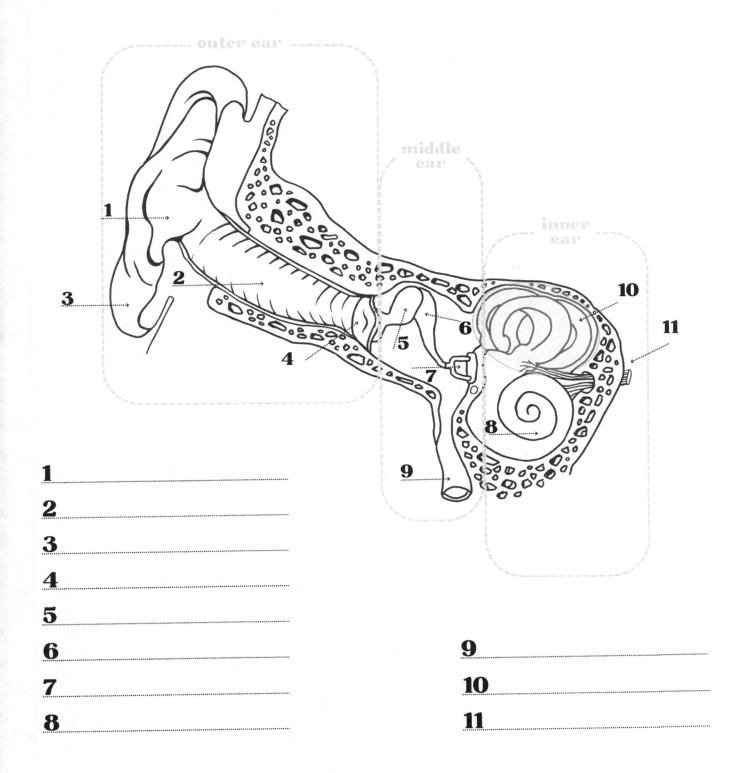

1 _____

2 _____

3 _____

4 _____

5 _____

6 _____

7 _____

8 _____

9 _____

10 _____

11 _____

Satisfaction Rating Scale
☹ ☹ 😐 🙂 😊

Page Revision Tracker
☐ ☐ ☐ ☐ ☐

1 - Lingual tonsil

2 - Circum lingual papillae

3 - Filiform lingual papillae

4 - Epiglottis

5 - Palatine tonsil

6 - Foramen Cecum

7 - Sulcum terminalis

8 - Median lingual sulcum

9 - Fungiform lingual papillae

10 - Apex

Sense of taste

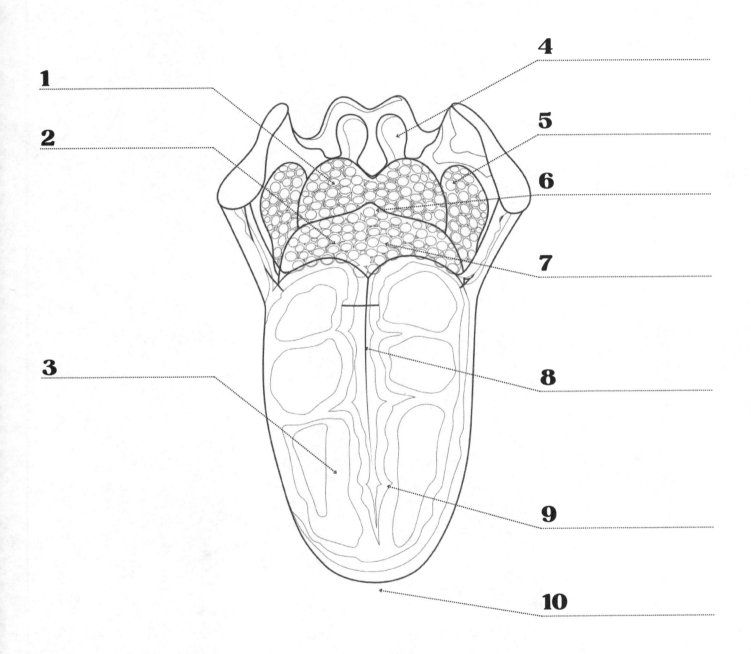

1

2

3

4

5

6

7

8

9

10

Satisfaction Rating Scale
☹ ☹ 😐 🙂 😊

Page Revision Tracker
☐ ☐ ☐ ☐ ☐

Key Word Index

Made in the USA
Las Vegas, NV
30 September 2024